# HOMEMADE FRENCH SAUCES

*Quick & Easy Dinner Sauces and Recipes*

*to make any meal lip-smacking*

BY DANIEL JAMES CHAMBERLIN

Copyright © 2012 Daniel James Chamberlin

All rights reserved. No part of this book may be reproduced, distributed or transmitted in any form or by any electronic or mechanical means without permission in writing from Daniel James Chamberlin.

Disclaimer: While all attempts have been made to verify information provided in this publication, the Author assumes no responsibility for errors, omissions or contrary interpretation of the subject matter herein.

ISBN: 1479259047
ISBN-13: 978-1479259045

Also check out

# THE HOMEMADE COOK: HOMEMADE ITALIAN SAUCES

available on Amazon.com!

# TABLE OF CONTENTS

**Forward** — 1

**Roux Sauces**

Béchamel (White Sauce) — 6

Soubise (Onion Sauce) — 8

Sauce aux Champignons (Mushroom Sauce) — 10

**Goes well with:**

Gratin Dauphinois — 14

Tomato and Mushroom Galette — 16

**Nouvelle Sauces**

Orange Gastrique (Sweet & Sour) — 20

Sauce Moutarde (Mustard Sauce) — 22

Sauce au Roquefort (Blue Cheese) — 24

**Goes well with:**

Crêpes aux Poireaux — 28

Chicken Cordon Bleu — 32

## Cold Sauces

Vinaigrette (Oil & Vinegar) — 36

Mayonnaise (Oil & Egg) — 38

Tomato Coulis — 40

### Goes well with:

Quiche Lorraine sans Pâte — 44

Fish en Papillote — 46

## Emulsified Sauces

Hollandaise (Butter & Egg) — 50

Béarnaise Sauce — 52

Burre Blanc (Butter & Wine) — 54

### Goes well with:

Asparagus Soufflé — 58

Eggs Benedict — 60

## Storage and Reheating of Sauces — 62

## Glossary — 66

## Recommended Reading — 72

*"Just speak very loudly and quickly, and state your position with utter conviction, as the French do, and you'll have a marvelous time"*

- Julia Child

# FORWARD

Ah, the French! Every culture in the world has sauces, but the French were the ones to turn sauce-making into an art form. Most of what we do today in the kitchen, most of the techniques and tools of the trade, come from France's rich culinary history. From the basics to sauces that served kings, the sauces presented in this book are practical, doable versions of venerable sauce classics.

The French kitchen does not hurry itself, and old-school recipes like those catalogued in Auguste Escoffier's *Le Guide Culinaire* sometimes took 2 or 3 days to make. I have opted towards practical concerns in this book, and have worked to balance tradition with more rapid, modern techniques to provide sauces that can be made quickly and easily in the home kitchen. While it was not possible to contain all of the myriad recipes of the sauces of France in one book, I believe the sauces here are representative of the flavors and traditions of France, both old and new.

Sauce gives flavor, and excitement, and punch. It makes good dishes better, and great dishes even greater. Better still, sauces can be added to anything that you feel like cooking, from simple dishes to fancy fare. This book takes a non-traditional look at sauces and turns the meal upside-down. Storable sauces, made fresh or in advance, take the center stage here. Everything that you make is going to be better.

Whether it's pan-fried fish fillets or just some grilled vegetables, you can serve it up with more style and flavor by adding sauce. If you're a meat-lover or if you're a vegetarian, the food you want to make is going to be better. It's a great way to cook something new every day. Or, cook the same dish and have the leftovers with different sauces, giving you totally different meals throughout the week and keeping you from getting hungry or bored.

The idea behind this book is to have maximum impact in your kitchen with sauces that require a minimum of training and a small list of ingredients. The point isn't to break the bank with exotic ingredients. It's to start using your kitchen, make better food than you can get at a drive-in window, and most of all, get you cooking.

So let's give it a shot!

# ROUX SAUCES

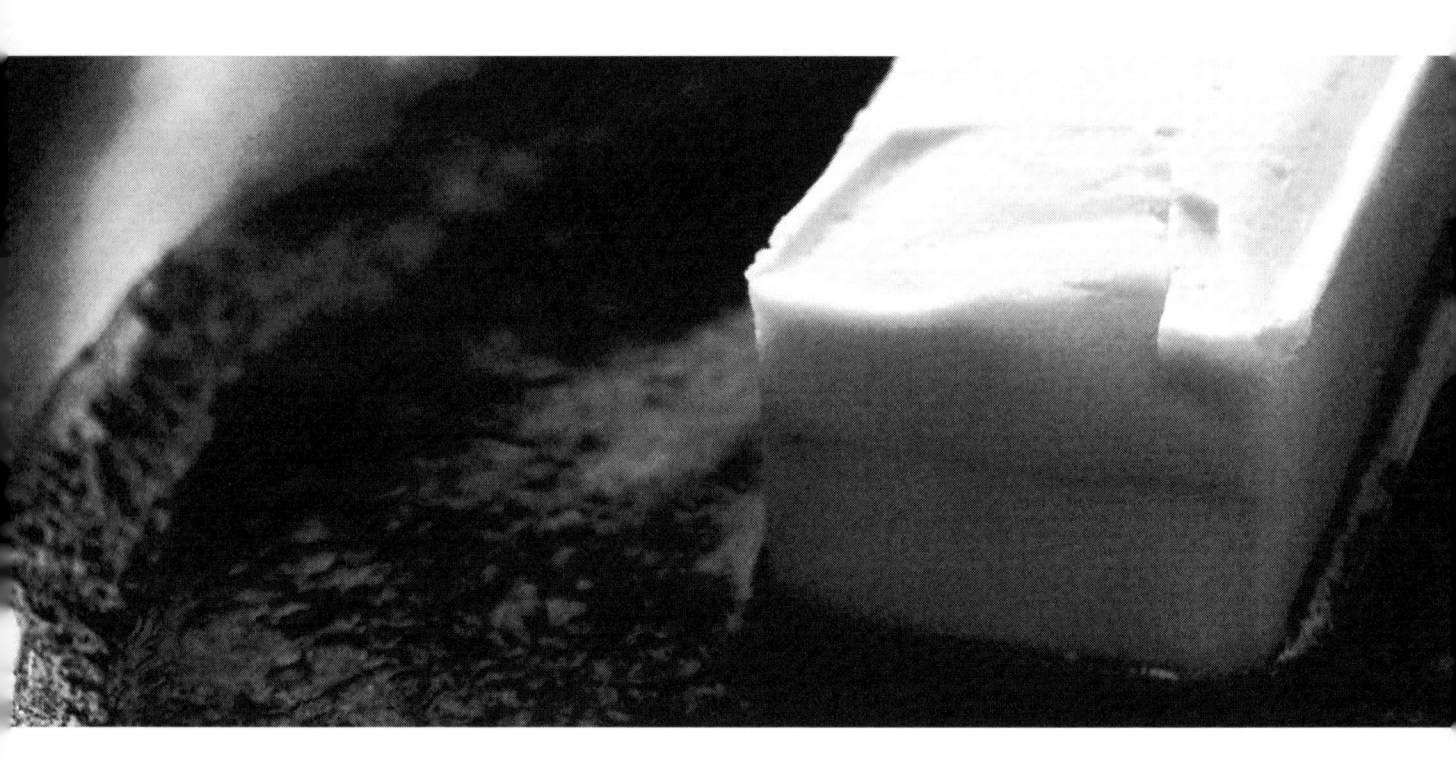

A *roux* is a mixture of fat and starch that acts as a thickener for other liquids. The fat used in a roux is traditionally butter, and the starch is usually white wheat flour. Roux sauces form the backbone of the traditional French kitchen, and they're perfect for the home cook since the technique in making them is always the same. The perfect roux was said to be made of equal parts *in weight* butter to flour. I've found that a simple 1 to 1 volume works more easily, so that's what the recipes in this book use.

Béchamel (beh-sha-mel) is the starting point for making roux sauces. It's so fundamental that it used to be taught in Home Economics classes in American schools (when they still had Home Ec) as *white sauce*. Since white sauce *(sauce blanche)* has another meaning as a different sauce in French, I'll keep saying béchamel. It's useful as a sauce on its own, as a base to make other sauces out of, and as a base in cooking other dishes: for gratins, mac and cheese, and other baked goods.

As with all Mother Sauces - and as the name indicates - there are many Child Sauces (also called Small Sauces) that are easily created once you have the basic recipe down. I'll mention some of these variations for these sauces as we go along, but once you have the hang of it you'll get bunches of ideas of your own for how the basic concept can be modified as you like.

I will mention beforehand that there is an ongoing and never-ending debate about the correct way to keep lumps out of a roux. Do you heat up the liquid to add it to a hot roux? Or do you add a cold liquid straight from the fridge? Or do you cool the roux and warm the liquid to room temperature? And on and on. While a lot of the opinions out there seem to be something akin to superstition, there is actual food science that explains the confusion. Without getting too far into it, the basic point is this: flour will clump if it contacts hot water. That's why you coat the flour in fat - melting the butter to coat the flour encases it in oil, which keeps the water from clumping the flour.

If the temperature is too low though, the butter will re-solidify and you'll get clumps. If it's too hot, the starch will seize and you'll get clumps. So, the easiest way to balance this out is with a simple idea: *hot* roux, *cold* liquid, or vice-versa. I use the hot roux, cold liquid method exclusively. I have found it to be the most reliable, problem-free method. I never run into clumps this way, but if that dreaded day should come, no worries, just throw it in a blender.

When reheating a roux sauce, adding a bit of the liquid you used to make it can help bring it all back together nicely.

Let's get to it!

# BÉCHAMEL
## (WHITE SAUCE)

## INGREDIENTS

*2 Tbsp* flour

*2 Tbsp* unsalted butter

*2 cups* milk

*1/4 tsp* ground nutmeg, preferably fresh

*1/2 tsp* salt

# PREPARATION

**1** Set a saucepan over low heat. Add the flour. This is backwards from how a roux is traditionally made, but it works better. Cut your butter into $1/2$ inch slices.

**2** Add one piece of the butter to the saucepan, whisking to combine it with the flour. When it melts, add another piece. Add one piece at a time after each one is melted and whisked in before adding the next one.

**3** When all of the butter has been added and whisked in, you should have a smooth paste. Cook it on low heat, stirring, for another minute or so, but don't let it brown. Prevent it from browning by keeping the heat low, stirring, and most of all by not cooking it for too long.

**4** Add the milk in a stream while whisking. Make sure that it is cold. This may be contrary to what you have heard, but don't worry, it will work. Hot roux, cold milk, no lumps. Once all the milk is in, raise the heat to medium.

**5** As you continue cooking, you'll notice the mixture thickening. As it cools, it will become thicker. When it coats a spoon, and a line drawn in that spoon with your finger keeps its shape, you're done. Add the salt and nutmeg.

**TIP:** Béchamel can be flavored any way that you can think of. Garlic and any herb you have handy are great ways to start. To make *Sauce Mornay*, popularly known as cheese sauce, simply trade out the seasoning and add about 2 ounces of your favorite cheese, shredded, to the mixture instead. The traditional choice would be half Gruyère and half Parmigiano-Reggiano.

# SAUCE SOUBISE
## (ONION SAUCE)

## INGREDIENTS

*2 Tbsp* flour

*4 Tbsp* unsalted butter

*1 cup* milk

*2 large* white onions, chopped

*½ tsp* salt

# PREPARATION

**1** In a saucepan over medium heat melt 2 Tbsp of the butter and cook the chopped onions in it.

**2** Cook until the onions are soft and translucent, but not yet browned. Put them into a food processor or blender, and purée. Set aside.

**3** In a clean saucepan over low heat, add the flour. Add the butter a piece at a time, whisking to mix into a paste. cook for a minute or two, stirring. This is to remove the raw flour taste from the roux.

**4** Add the milk while whisking. Cold milk, hot roux. Turn up to medium or medium-high.

**5** When the mixture coats a spoon and a line drawn on the spoon with your finger holds its shape, add the onion purée. Whisk to combine.

**TIP:** Add about 1/4 cup of grated cheese when adding the onion purée for added richness.

# SAUCE AUX CHAMPIGNONS
## (MUSHROOM SAUCE)

## INGREDIENTS

*4 Tbsp* unsalted butter

*2 Tbsp* flour

*½ cup* white wine

*1 cup* chicken stock

*½ cup* heavy cream

*1 cup* mushrooms, sliced

*1 small* shallot, minced

# PREPARATION

**1** In a heavy-bottomed saucepan over medium heat, melt 2 Tbsp of the butter and wait until it starts to get bubbly. Add the shallot and mushrooms, and cook until soft, about 5 minutes.

**2** Add the chicken stock and white wine. Turn up the heat to medium-high. Continue cooking until the liquids are reduced by half, about 10-15 minutes. Lower heat to medium.

**3** Add the other 2 Tbsp of butter. Once it's melted, sprinkle the flour around the pan and stir it in. Continue cooking for about 5 minutes. The sauce will thicken.

**4** Add the heavy cream. Cook for a few more minutes, and turn the heat off. Add the unsalted butter, and stir until it melts into the sauce, making it glossy. It probably won't need salt, but you can add some to taste if you like.

**TIP:** Crimini or button mushrooms are always a good bet, but you can really get some interesting flavors out of shiitake or other mushroom varieties as well.

# RECIPE RECOMMENDATIONS

The roux sauces here are great with starches like pasta, potatoes, and breads. They work well with hardy vegetables, and in macaroni, gratins, casseroles, and other baked dishes. Roux sauces can be flavored any which way, and the roux itself can also be cooked a bit longer to make a brown roux, which is nutty and rich.

# GRATIN DAUPHINOIS

## INGREDIENTS

*2 lbs* potatoes

*1 cup* grated cheese, preferably Gruyère

*1-2 Tbsp* unsalted butter

*1 clove* garlic

*2 cups* any Homemade Sauces roux sauce recipe

*to taste* salt and pepper

# PREPARATION

**1** Preheat the oven to 425 F. Reheat the *Homemade Sauces* roux sauce *(see Storage and Reheating of Sauces)*. Peel the potatoes, and slice them as thinly as you can.

**2** Cut the clove of garlic in half. Rub a baking dish with the garlic. Butter the dish with the butter.

**3** Arrange half of the sliced potatoes in the buttered dish. Season with salt and pepper. Pour half of the *Homemade Sauces* roux sauce over the potatoes, and sprinkle with half of the grated cheese.

**4** Arrange the remaining sliced potatoes on top. Season with a bit more salt and pepper. Pour the rest of the *Homemade Sauces* roux sauce over the potatoes, and finish by sprinkling the remaining grated cheese on top.

**5** Bake uncovered in the oven until the top is browned and bubbling, about 20-25 minutes. Best served warm.

**TIP:** Try gratin with other hardy vegetables in place of the potatoes, like fennel bulbs or cauliflower.

# TOMATO AND MUSHROOM GALETTE

## INGREDIENTS

**For the dough:**

*1 cup* all-purpose flour

*8 Tbsp (1 stick)* unsalted butter

*about $1/3$ cup* ice-cold water

*$1/2$ tsp* salt

**For the filling:**

*1-2 medium* tomatoes, sliced

*3-4* crimini mushrooms, quartered

*1 cup* any Homemade Sauces roux sauce recipe

# PREPARATION

**1**   Put the flour and salt into a food processor or blender. Pulse a few times. Cut the butter into 1/2 inch slices. Add to the processor or blender 1 slice at a time, pulsing to combine.

**2**   When the mixture resembles coarse cereal start adding the ice water. You can make ice water by melting a few cubes of ice into room temperature water. You may not need all of the water, or you may need more, depending on heat and elevation. Add enough so that the mixture just comes together into a dough, but no more.

**3**   Bring the dough together into a ball, and flatten it somewhat into a thick disc. Wrap the dough in plastic wrap and put it in the refrigerator for about an hour.

**4**   Preheat the oven to 375 F. Roll out the dough into a roughly round shape 1/8 inch thick. It should be around 12-14 inches in diameter.

**5**   Spoon the *Homemade Sauces* roux sauce evenly over the dough, leaving about 2 inches around the edges clear. Top with the tomato slices and mushrooms.

**6**   Going around in a circle, fold a few inches of the edges of the dough inwards, leaving the center uncovered. 5 or 6 folds should do it, and it looks kind of like a pinwheel. Bake in the oven until the pastry is golden brown, 35-40 minutes.

**TIP:**   Galettes are like pizzas: you can put whatever you like on them! Try your favorite combinations of vegetables, or use fruit for a dessert version.

# NOUVELLE SAUCES

Nouvelle Cuisine was a culinary movement that replaced roux in their dishes with other ways of thickening their sauces: mostly with reductions, cold butter, and cream. Beurre Blanc is the poster child of this style, but I've included that sauce in the Emulsified Sauces section (where it reveals its true nature). Some of the other sauces to come out of this style - reductions like gastrique and simpler ways of handling traditional sauces, like sauce moutarde - show the ingenuity and creativity that the Nouvelle style produced.

The sauces here are representative of the style but vary greatly from each other in composition. If I had to say what the common link between them was, I would say it's their boldness in flavor and their fearlessness in being what they are. I would also risk saying that they are unfetteringly French in bearing, and in flavor. Below is a brief description of the three distinct flavors that we'll go over:

*Gastrique* is the French version of a sweet and sour sauce. It was originally used as a technique for adding depth to the flavor of other sauces, but over time it's become a sauce in its own right. Fruit and sugar produces the sweet; vinegar the sour. There are unlimited variations that can be made simply by switching out which fruit and which vinegar you use. Traditionally, fresh fruit is cooked down with sugar before adding the vinegar, but I have a wonderful shortcut: start with jam or fruit preserves. This not only gives you what you need - sweetened, softened fruit - it also thickens the sauce more quickly and makes trying a new flavor as simple as choosing a different jam.

Mustard has always been an unwaveringly reliable French product. I'm not sure if technically I can credit the French with the invention of mustard - that was probably the Romans - but I do know that the city of Dijon was already famous as a mustard epicenter by the 13th century. You can't argue with that much history: Dijon mustard is definitely what I recommend using in these sauces. French mustards have vinegar in them, and that mellows out the bite of the mustard seeds, which is great for a smooth flavored sauce.

*Roquefort* cheese, probably the most famous blue cheese, is made in Roquefort-sur-Soulzon in southern France. It is so famous for this type of cheese that what we call blue cheese is often simply called Roquefort in Europe. The French are known for their strong cheeses, and this smoky, tangy variety has a wonderful flavor on meats and hardy starches like potatoes.

Let's get cooking!

# ORANGE GASTRIQUE
## (SWEET & SOUR)

## INGREDIENTS

*2 Tbsp* unsalted butter

*½ cup* orange marmalade

*1 medium* orange, juice and zest

*4 Tbsp* white wine vinegar

*1 small* shallot, minced

*¼ tsp* salt

# PREPARATION

**1** In a saucepan over medium-low heat, melt the unsalted butter. Add the shallow and cook until translucent, about 5 minutes.

**2** Add the orange marmalade, orange juice, 1-2 tsp of the orange zest, and white wine vinegar to the pan. Raise the heat to medium-high until the mixture starts bubbling, then reduce heat to low and simmer for 5-10 minutes. You can substitute $1/4$ cup orange juice for the orange.

**3** Purée the mixture in a blender or food processor. Add the salt. The gastrique will thicken as it cools down.

**TIP:** Try mixing and matching different jams with different vinegars and you'll find many possibilities with this easy technique.

# SAUCE MOUTARDE
## (MUSTARD SAUCE)

## INGREDIENTS

*2 Tbsp* unsalted butter

*½ cup* dry white wine

*¼ cup* Dijon mustard

*½ cup* heavy cream

*1 large* shallot, minced

*1 clove* garlic, minced

*2 Tbsp* flat-leaf parsley, chopped

*¼ tsp* salt

# PREPARATION

**1**     Put a frying pan over medium-low heat. Add the butter and wait until it becomes frothy. Add the minced shallot and cook until translucent, about 5 minutes.

**2**     Add the garlic and white wine. Bring to a boil over high heat, then lower the heat to medium-high and cook the liquid to reduce it until syrupy, about 3 minutes.

**3**     Add the mustard and the cream. Continue cooking over medium-high heat for another 5 minutes. The sauce will thicken.

**4**     When the sauce has thickened enough to hold a line drawn through it with the back of a spoon (wooden spoon if you're on non-stick!), add the chopped fresh parsley and salt, and turn off the heat.

**TIP:**     The quality of the mustard really makes a difference in this one. Go for a good Dijon brand, something like *Maille*. Also, try making this sauce in the same pan if you've just cooked some meat - the flavor will be much richer, but the shelf life will go down a bit.

# SAUCE AU ROQUEFORT
## (BLUE CHEESE SAUCE)

## INGREDIENTS

*3-4 ounces* blue cheese, crumbled

*3 Tbsp* unsalted butter

*3 Tbsp* dry white wine

*1 large* shallot, minced

*1 cup* heavy cream

*1/4 tsp* pepper, preferably white

# PREPARATION

**1**     Add the butter to a saucepan over medium-low heat, and cook the shallot until translucent, about 5 minutes.

**2**     Add the white wine. Add the crumbled blue cheese, and mash it in with a spoon or spatula. Stir the cheese in until it has melted.

**3**     Add the heavy cream. Cook on medium until the sauce coats a spoon, and a line drawn on the spoon with your finger keeps its shape, about 5 minutes.

**4**     Turn off the heat and add the pepper. You probably won't need salt because of the cheese, but salt to taste if you like.

**TIP:**     If blue cheese is not your thing, consider making this sauce with a grated hard cheese; though I think you may change your mind if you try this version over a steak or some potatoes.

# RECIPE RECOMMENDATIONS

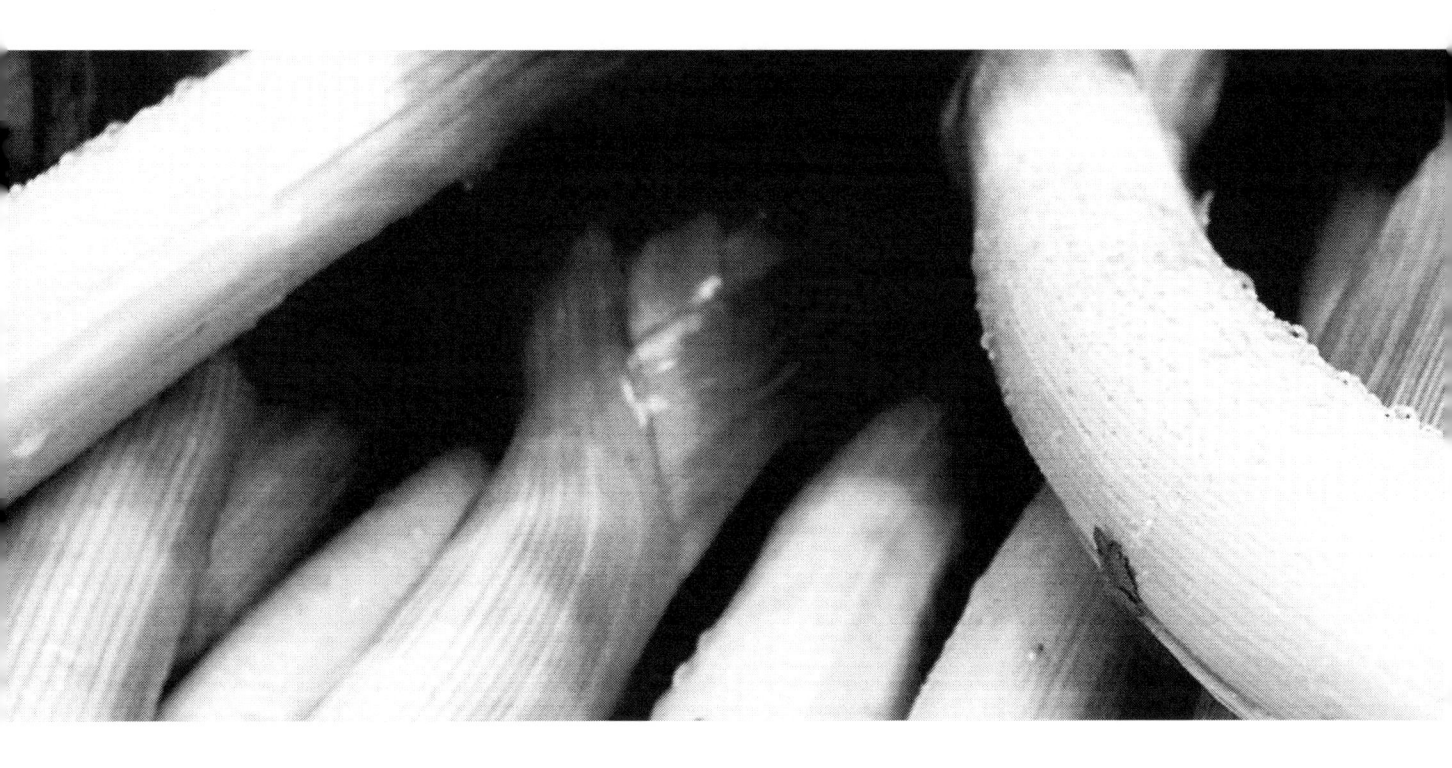

Nouvelle sauces can be powerful and eclectic, and usually a little goes a long way. Try berry gastrique on poultry and game, dark cherry on ham or turkey, or tangerine with seafood. Mustard sauces are great with meats and chicken, potatoes, eggs, and greens. Blue cheese is excellent on steaks. Experiment a bit and these sauces can go a long way.

# CRÊPES AUX POIREAUX
## (CREPES WITH LEEKS)

## INGREDIENTS

*1 cup* flour

*2 large* eggs

*4 Tbsp* unsalted butter

*1/2 cup* milk

*1/2 cup* water

*1/4 tsp* coarse salt

*1 large* leek

*2-3 Tbsp* oil, olive or vegetable

*1 cup* any The Homemade Cook Nouvelle sauce recipe

# PREPARATION

**1**   In a saucepan over low heat, melt 2 Tbsp of the butter until frothy. Put the melted butter, the flour, the eggs, the milk, the water, and the coarse salt into a blender or food processor. Blend on medium for around 30 seconds. Shut off the blender, scrape down the sides with a spatula, then blend again on high for about 30 seconds. Put the batter mixture in a bowl and refrigerate for at least 1 hour. This can also be done with a mixer.

**2**   Cut off the green top parts of the leek. You can make stock or soup out of these but they're usually too woody and fibrous to eat. Slice leek down its entire length and clean out the inside thoroughly with running water. Leeks have a tendency to collect dirt and sand; make sure you get it all out. Chop the leek into $1/2$ inch pieces.

**3**   In a saucepan over medium-low heat, melt the remaining 2 Tbsp of butter and wait until its frothy. Add the sliced leek and cook until tender, about 5-7 minutes. Set aside.

**4**   To make the crêpes, put a small frying pan over medium-high heat. Add a little bit of the oil, just enough to coat the pan. Pour about $1/4$ cup of batter at a time in the center of the pan. Move and tilt the pan with a circular motion so that the batter coats the bottom evenly.

**5**   Cook each crêpe until the bottom is light brown, about 2 minutes. Loosen by shaking the pan or with a spatula, and turn over to cook the other side. This side will be faster: about 1 minute. Put the crêpe on a plate, and repeat with the rest of the batter, stacking the crêpes up. A piece of wax paper in between each crêpe is useful to keep them from sticking to each other.

**6**   Reheat the *Homemade Sauces* Nouvelle sauce ***(see Storage and Reheating of Sauces)***. Add the cooked leek to the sauce. Stir to combine.

**7**     Take each crêpe, pour 1-2 Tbsp of the leek and sauce mixture in the middle, fold in half, and then in half again. Can be served warm or cold.

**TIP:**     The fillings that you can use for crêpe are limitless. Pick your favorite meat, seafood, cheese, or vegetable and combine it with a *Homemade Sauces* sauce to find your favorites.

# CHICKEN CORDON BLEU

## INGREDIENTS

*4 (6-8 oz each)* boneless, skinless chicken breasts

*4-8 thin slices* ham

*1 cup* shredded cheese, preferably Swiss

*1 cup* breadcrumbs

*¼ cup* flour

*1 Tbsp* unsalted butter

*1 large* egg

*A pinch* salt and pepper

*¼ - ½ cup* any The Homemade Cook Nouvelle sauce recipe

# PREPARATION

**1** Preheat the oven to 350 F. Butter a baking pan with the butter. Place the chicken breasts, one at a time, between 2 sheets of plastic wrap. Pound them to an even thickness of around $1/4$ inch with a meat pounder or rolling pin.

**2** Season the pounded chicken breasts on both sides with the salt and pepper. Place 1 or 2 slices of ham on each breast, and top with $1/4$ of the shredded cheese.

**3** Roll up the chicken breasts one at a time and stick a toothpick in them to keep the pinwheel shape together. Put them on a plate so that they are not touching each other.

**4** Sprinkle the pinwheels all over with the flour. Crack the egg into a bowl and beat it together. Coat each pinwheel in egg. Sprinkle the breadcrumbs all over the pinwheels.

**5** Arrange the pinwheels in the baking pan so that they aren't touching. Bake in the oven until the chicken is done (the juices should be running clear), about 30-35 minutes. While this is baking, reheat the *Homemade Sauces* Nouvelle sauce *(see Storage and Reheating of Sauces)*.

**6** Remove from the oven, top with the *Homemade Sauces* Nouvelle sauce, and serve. You can also spoon the sauce onto the plate first, and set each pinwheel on top to create a nice looking dish.

**TIP:** One easy method to ensure that chicken is cooked through is to poke the thickest part of the meat with a knife. Juices will begin to flow. If they are clear, the chicken is done. If they are pink or reddish, continue cooking until they come out clear.

# COLD SAUCES

Not all sauces need to be hot. Cold sauces are simple and quick to prepare, and make excellent dressings and ingredients as well as fine sauces. The sauces presented here are ones we often find ourselves buying in the store, but you'll never want to go back once you find out how easy and delicious they are when made at home.

Vinaigrette is an oil and vinegar emulsion. It's an obvious go-to for your salads, but beyond its use as a dressing, I want you to recognize this wonderful cold emulsion as a marinade and sauce as well. You can vary it up a ton just by switching around which oil and which vinegar you use.

Mayonnaise is a lot like hollandaise: it is a yolk-based emulsion. The main difference is in the fat used: while hollandaise relies on butter, mayonnaise uses oil. Contrary to what seems to be popular belief, the French are not adamant about what oil you use - olive, safflower, grapeseed, vegetable, or even a mixture works fine. Use the oil you're comfortable with, or the one you have on hand. That goes for vinaigrettes, as well.

Ah yes, the question of raw yolks. The real but incredibly tiny risk of sickness caused by salmonella can be minimized by using fresh, clean eggs from a quality producer, and by not letting the yolk touch the outside of the egg shell. But I have to be blunt here: if you assume your food is poisonous, you should really be buying from someone else. Raw eggs have been eaten world-wide for a very, very long time. Get in touch with a local producer that you trust, and don't spend your time worrying.

# VINAIGRETTE
## (OIL & VINEGAR)

## INGREDIENTS

*½ cup*  oil, olive or vegetable

*2 Tbsp*  wine vinegar

*1 tsp*  Dijon mustard

*1 small*  shallot

*1-2 sprigs*  flat-leaf parsley, chopped

*¼ tsp*  coarse salt

# PREPARATION

**1** After mincing the shallot, place it in a non-metal bowl with the vinegar and the salt. Let it sit for a few minutes.

**2** Add the Dijon mustard, and mix until smooth. Add the chopped parsley.

**3** Transfer everything to a mixer, blender, or food processor that has an opening you can pour though. On medium speed, add the oil in a slow steady stream. You can add additional salt or herbs to taste.

**TIP:** For the wine vinegar, you have lots of options. White, red, sherry, and champagne will all give you different vinaigrettes to try!

# MAYONNAISE
## (OIL & EGG)

## INGREDIENTS

*1 large* egg

*2 Tbsp* vinegar, preferably white wine

*½ tsp* Dijon mustard

*½ tsp* coarse salt

*1 cup* oil, vegetable or olive

# PREPARATION

**1** Put the egg, the vinegar, the Dijon mustard, and the coarse salt in a blender or food processor (you can also use an inversion blender or mixer in a bowl). Blend on medium until the color becomes pale, about 30 seconds. Stop blending.

**2** Put the blender on low and leave it running. Add the oil 1 Tbsp at a time, very slowly, in a steady stream. After about 3 Tbsp, you can start to pour the rest of the oil in, but do it slowly.

**3** The mixture should both whiten and visibly thicken. Once all the oil is blended in, you are good to go.

**TIP:** Use fresh eggs of the best quality that you can find, and store unused mayonnaise in the refrigerator. If you want a tangier flavor, use lemon juice in place of the vinegar. If you want to try Japanese style mayonnaise, use apple cider vinegar. You can also make tartar sauce by adding chopped pickles, capers, and onion.

# TOMATO COULIS

## INGREDIENTS

*4 medium*  tomatoes, peels removed

*3 Tbsp*  olive oil

*1 large*  shallot, minced

*1 clove*  garlic, smashed

*1 pinch*  cayenne

*½ tsp*  coarse salt

# PREPARATION

**1**   To remove the tomato peels, make 2 cuts forming an X on the bottom of each tomato, and poach them in boiling water for about 30 seconds.

**2**   Cut the tomatoes into quarters and scrape out the seeds. It doesn't have to be perfect, just scrape most of them out with your knife or a spoon. Chop them up; it can be rough.

**3**   Put the chopped tomatoes, the minced shallot, the garlic, the cayenne, and the coarse salt into a blender or food processor. Pulse until the ingredients are combined. Add the oil, and blend on low until smooth. If you want to go the extra mile, you can force it through a sieve, making it extra shiny.

**TIP:**   Coulis can be made out of other vegetables or fruit as well. A classic dessert coulis is made from raspberries, sugar, and lemon juice. If using berries, you definitely want to strain the sauce through a fine mesh to remove the seeds.

# RECIPE RECOMMENDATIONS

Cold sauces go well with steamed vegetables and fish, salads, and greens. Warmed up, they go well with meats, chicken, and potatoes. Coulis is really good with aubergine (eggplant) and with pasta or fish. You can use peeled roasted red bell peppers in place of tomatoes to make a red pepper coulis. Mayonnaise can be made into *Sauce Rémoulade* with the addition of mustard, pickles, capers, and herbs like parsley, chervil, and tarragon. Vinaigrette can be something new each time with different combinations of herbs. After trying the recipes here, switch it up and use the techniques with different vegetables and herbs.

# QUICHE LORRAINE SANS PÂTE
## (CRUSTLESS)

## INGREDIENTS

*8 slices* bacon

*4 large* eggs

*2 cups* shredded cheese, preferably Swiss

*2 Tbsp* onion, minced

*2-3 Tbsp* flour

*1 Tbsp* unsalted butter

*1 cup* heavy cream

*1 cup* milk

*1 cup* any Homemade Sauces cold sauce recipe

# PREPARATION

**1** Butter a 10 inch pie pan or dish. Sprinkle the flour around the dish evenly. Preheat the oven to 425 F.

**2** Cut the bacon into small pieces. In a skillet over medium-high heat, cook the bacon with the minced onion, stirring occasionally. Cook until the onion is translucent, about 5 minutes.

**3** Add the bacon and onion mixture to the pie dish, but don't add the bacon fat from the pan. Sprinkle the cheese around evenly. Pour the milk mixture on top.

**4** Bake in the oven until set, 20-25 minutes. Top with the remaining *Homemade Sauces* cold sauce.

**TIP:** You can add a crust to this recipe for a more traditional *Quiche Lorraine*, or keep it simple as in this recipe. Quiche is also quite often made with a roux sauce as its base.

# FISH EN PAPILLOTE

## INGREDIENTS

*4 fillets*  white fish (4-6 oz each, such as sole, snapper, or halibut)

*1-2 Tbsp*  unsalted butter

*1 small*  lemon

*1/2 cup*  carrot, julienned or shredded

*A pinch*  salt and pepper

*1/2 cup*  any Homemade Sauces cold sauce recipe

# PREPARATION

**1** Preheat the oven to 400 degrees F. Cut 4 pieces of aluminum foil large enough to wrap around each fillet.

**2** Season each fillet on both sides with salt and pepper. Place each fillet in the center of each piece of foil.

**3** Pour ¼ of the *Homemade Sauces* cold sauce on each fillet. Top each with ¼ of the julienned or shredded carrot, ¼ of the butter, and a squeeze of lemon juice.

**4** Fold the aluminum foil over each fillet and seal tightly. Use another piece of foil if you need to. Bake in the oven until the fish is cooked through, about 12-15 minutes.

**5** You can open the packets, called *papillotes*, in advance, or you can serve them that way at the table to keep them warm.

**TIP:** The traditional recipe for cooking *en Papillote* uses parchment paper, but aluminum foil is far more convenient and easy to work with.

# EMULSIFIED SAUCES

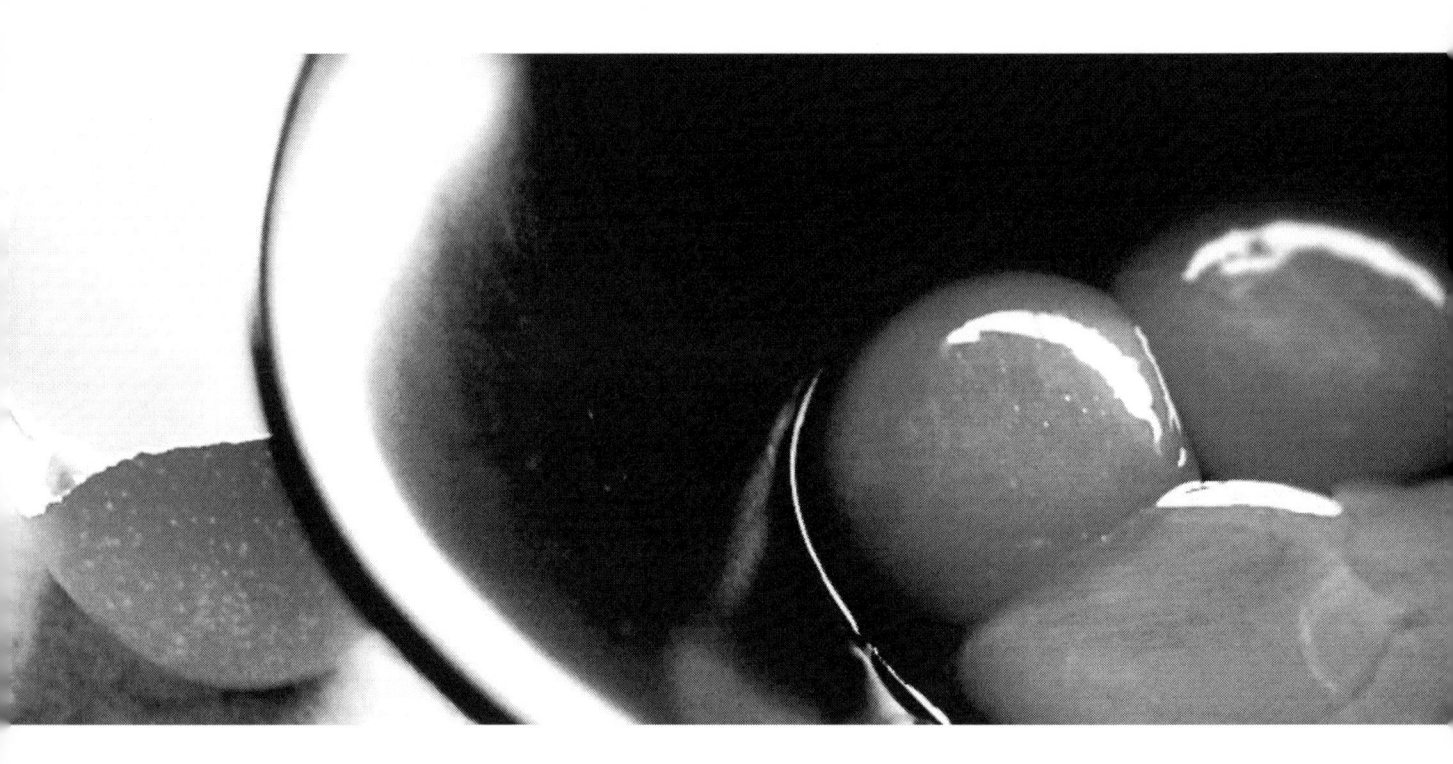

Emulsions are mixtures that have one ingredient suspended in another, in thousands or millions of tiny droplets. Usually, like with water and oil, these two don't get along, but emulsions have a third element, an emulsifier (think relationship counselor) that has the two getting together like old pals. Egg yolk is one of the most reliable such counselors, but many others, like mustard and even garlic, are out there helping the kitchen come together, one colloid matrix at a time.

*Sauce Hollandaise* is the mother sauce of this category, immortalized on the American menu for its starring role in Eggs Benedict. Like all mother sauces, there are many hollandaise derivatives, some of which I will have time to present here. I am also including the Nouvelle-styled *beurre blanc* here, since it is a true emulsion and requires the same attention in preparation.

There are a couple of reasons why a sauce like hollandaise, the prime representative of this group of sauces, is feared by would-be cooks in the kitchen. Egg yolk coagulates (coagulate just means to change to a solid state) at around 150 F, so too hot and you're scrambled. Butter has the opposite problem: it will re-solidify at room temperature, so too cold is no good. What's a home cook to do?

Anything with a sweet spot like that seems to instill people with a special fear that they'll screw up, but the recipes here will get you over that. I've opted away from pure tradition for the sake of practical, doable sauces that you'll find impress your dinner guests far more than they should, but then, they're still afraid of attempting to make hollandaise, aren't they?

# HOLLANDAISE
## (BUTTER & EGG)

## INGREDIENTS

*½ cup (1 stick)* unsalted butter

*2 large* egg yolks

*1 Tbsp* lemon juice

*½ tsp* coarse salt

*1 pinch* cayenne powder

# PREPARATION

**1** Add the butter to a small saucepan over low heat. Melt the butter and wait until it's frothy, but don't let it brown. Turn off the heat.

**2** Put the egg yolks, the lemon juice, the coarse salt, and the cayenne powder into a blender or food processor. Blend at medium speed until the mixture lightens in color, about 10 seconds.

**3** Turn the blender down to its lowest speed. While the blender is running, slowly pour in the melted butter in a thin stream. You can leave the last bit of butter froth in the pan, those are milk solids. It will thicken very quickly. Once all the butter is blended in, turn off the blender or food processor.

**4** Taste, and add additional lemon juice, salt, or cayenne as you like. Hollandaise likes to be warm, but doesn't like extreme temperatures very much. You can keep the blender container in a pot of warm water while serving to keep it warm.

**TIP:** Once refrigerated or frozen, hollandaise is likely to split (separate) upon being reheated. Don't worry! After reheating, stir the broken hollandaise and add about 1 Tbsp of the mixture to a blender or food processor. Add 1 Tbsp of warm water and blend them together on low for a few seconds. Slowly add the rest of the broken mixture, and it will come back together. It's not as unforgiving as people would have you believe.

# BÉARNAISE

## INGREDIENTS

*2-3 large*  egg yolks

*3/4 cup*  unsalted butter

*1/2 cup*  white wine vinegar

*1 small*  shallot, minced

*2 cups*  fresh tarragon

*1/2 tsp*  coarse salt

# PREPARATION

**1** Cut the stocks off of the tarragon, and set them aside with half of the leaves. Chop the remaining tarragon leaves up roughly. Set the chopped leaves aside somewhere else.

**2** Set a saucepan over medium heat. Add the white wine vinegar along with the minced shallot, tarragon stocks, and whole tarragon leaves. Save the chopped leaves for later. Cook the liquid to reduce it by about half, then set aside to cool. This is now tarragon vinegar.

**3** In another saucepan over low heat, melt the butter. Wait until it is frothy, but don't let it brown. Turn off the heat.

**4** Put the egg yolks, the cooled vinegar mixture, and the coarse salt into a blender or food processor. Blend at medium speed until the mixture lightens in color, about 10 seconds. Turn off the blender, and put in the chopped tarragon leaves.

**5** Turn the blender on low. While the blender is running, slowly pour in the hot melted butter in a thin stream. You can leave the last bit of butter froth in the pan, those are milk solids. As you pour in the butter, the sauce will thicken. Once all the butter is blended in, turn off the blender or food processor.

**6** Taste, and add additional salt as you like. Béarnaise is like hollandaise: it likes to be warm, but doesn't like extreme temperatures very much. You can keep the blender container in a pot of warm water while serving to keep it warm.

**TIP:** If you make extra tarragon vinegar, you can keep it on hand to skip a few steps in making béarnaise, and to use in other dishes when they call for vinegar or lemon juice.

# BEURRE BLANC
## (BUTTER & WINE)

## INGREDIENTS

*1 cup (2 sticks)* unsalted butter, cold

*½ cup* dry white wine

*⅓ cup* heavy cream

*1 large* shallot, minced

*½ tsp* salt

# PREPARATION

**1** In a saucepan over high heat, add the shallot and white wine. Reduce until there is about 2 or 3 tablespoons worth. It will become somewhat syrupy.

**2** Add cream. When it begins to bubble, reduce the heat to low. Cut pieces, $1/2$ inch or so, of cold butter, and add them one at a time to the pan. Whisk in until each one melts before adding another. Cold from the refrigerator is best: the coldness of the butter thickens the sauce.

**3** When all the butter is added and whisked in, add the salt. Best served warm, since the butter will re-solidify if it cools off too much.

**TIP:** If you make this sauce with red wine instead of white wine, it will become a *Beurre Rouge*. A dry red wine, like a Cabernet Sauvignon or Merlot, is best, and it will go well with red meats.

# RECIPE RECOMMENDATIONS

Emulsified sauces contain plenty of butter, and go exceptionally well with eggs, asparagus, and salmon. They also go well with other fish, light meats, and poultry, and it helps to add some flavors like dill and capers for fish. Try different herbs to match your dish. I also find them well suited to savory baked goods.

# ASPARAGUS SOUFFLÉ

## INGREDIENTS

*1 bunch (about 10 oz)* asparagus

*2 Tbsp* flour

*1-2 Tbsp* unsalted butter

*½ cup* milk

*1 tsp* vinegar

*4 large* eggs

*½ cup* grated Gruyère cheese

*½ tsp* salt

*½ cup* any Homemade Sauces emulsified sauce recipe

# PREPARATION

**1** Preheat oven to 350 F. Butter 6 ramekins, or one round baking dish. Flour the buttered ramekins, and shake and tap the bottoms to get the excess flour out.

**2** Fill a pot about ¾ full of water, salt the water, and bring to a boil. Reheat the *Homemade Sauces* emulsified sauce *(see Storage and Reheating of Sauces)*, recombine it if it splits.

**3** Cut the asparagus into 1 inch pieces. Blanch the asparagus in the boiling water for about 2 minutes. Run under cold water for a bit to set the color, and then strain.

**4** Separate the eggs. Set the egg whites aside in a clean bowl. Make sure there's no yolk in there. Put the yolks into a blender or food processor along with the asparagus, the milk, the grated cheese, the reheated *Homemade Sauces* emulsified sauce, and the salt. Blend until smooth.

**5** Add the vinegar to the egg whites. Whip the whites until they form soft peaks. Fold the egg whites into the asparagus mixture, and don't over-mix: streaks of white are totally fine.

**6** Bake in the oven until puffed and golden brown, about 30 minutes. Serve with some more of the *Homemade Sauces* emulsified sauce you used on top if you like.

**TIP:** All soufflés fall when they cool, so don't worry too much about it. You can minimize falling by cooking at a lower oven temperature, like I've done in this recipe, and also by not opening the oven while it's still baking. If you really want the puff-up, make sure to serve it hot from the oven!

# EGGS BENEDICT

## INGREDIENTS

**2** English muffins

**4 large** eggs

**8 slices** bacon or ham

**1 pinch** sea salt

**2 Tbsp** white vinegar

**³/₄ cup** any Homemade Sauces emulsified sauce recipe

# PREPARATION

**1** Cook the bacon or ham in a fry pan. Go for tender instead of crisp. You won't need oil for bacon. Set aside.

**2** Fill a pot ¾ full of water. Bring to a boil. Turn down the heat until the water is bubbling gently. Add the vinegar.

**3** Break each egg one at a time into a ladle and carefully lower them into the bubbling water. Wait for 10-20 seconds for the egg white to start to take shape before you ease it out of the ladle. Continue putting one egg at a time in the water. The water should stay at a gentle bubble.

**4** Poach each egg for about 4 minutes; a little longer if you don't want the egg to be runny. Runny is better. Remove the poached eggs with a slotted spoon. Place them in a colander or in a bowl with a paper towel at the bottom. Keep them warm with a kitchen towel over the top.

**5** If using a previously made sauce, put the *Homemade Sauces* emulsified sauce into a ziplock bag. Squeeze out most of the air, seal the bag tightly, and put it into the pot of bubbling water. Heat through for about 2-3 minutes, until warm.

**6** Toast the English muffins. Put some bacon or ham on one half of an English muffin, top with a poached egg, pour over some of the *Homemade Sauces* emulsified sauce, and sprinkle on a little salt. Serve as soon as you can: it's best warm.

**TIP:** A popular vegetarian version of this dish can be made by substituting fresh avocado for the cooked bacon or ham.

# STORAGE AND REHEATING OF SAUCES

## STORAGE

**Freezer Bag Method**

Allow the sauce to cool in a bowl for at least 10 minutes, but for no more than 2 hours. Around room temperature is ideal. Put the sauce into a ziplock freezer bag, remove as much air from the bag as you can, and store in the refrigerator or freezer. This method makes it very easy to reheat the sauce.

Stored this way, the sauce will last for up to 1 week in the refrigerator*, or up to 3 months in the freezer.

*\* Hollandaise and other yolk-based sauces should not be stored in the refrigerator for more than 2 days.*

**Frozen Stock Cube Method**

Allow the sauce to cool in a bowl for at least 10 minutes, but for no more than 2 hours. Around room temperature is ideal. Pour the sauce into a cleaned, empty ice cube tray, and place in the freezer. These can be used like stock cubes, and make the sauce easier to portion out.

Kept this way, the sauce will last for up to 3 months stored in the freezer. To prevent freezer burn, place the ice cube tray itself inside a large ziplock freezer bag after the sauce has cooled.

# REHEATING

**To Reheat from a Freezer Bag**

Add enough water to a pot to cover the freezer bag, and bring it to a boil. Lower the heat to a gentle bubble, and put the freezer bag containing the sauce in the water. Make sure the bag is sealed completely. The sauce will be reheated and ready to use in about 3 minutes. Remove with tongs.

**To Reheat from a Frozen Stock Cube**

Place a saucepot on medium heat. Add the frozen stock cubes in the quantity required, along with 1-2 teaspoons of water*. Stir the cubes as they melt back into a sauce. When the sauce bubbles throughout, it is reheated and ready to use.**

*For Hollandaise and other yolk-based sauces, direct heat will cause the egg yolk to coagulate. Instead of putting the sauce cubes directly into a saucepot, seal them in a freezer bag and follow the To Reheat from a Freezer Bag instructions.*

**For all emulsified sauces, there is a possibility that they will split when reheated. To re-emulsify, stir the reheated broken sauce and add about 1 Tbsp of it to a blender or food processor. Add 1 Tbsp of warm water and blend together on low for a few seconds. With the blender still running, slowly add the rest of the broken mixture, and it will come back together. You can also do this with a whisk or hand mixer. If you are still having troubles bringing it together, one fresh yolk added with the warm water will increase the chances of re-emulsification even more.*

# GLOSSARY

**Boil**

When water reaches 100 degrees C (212 F), it boils. A *rolling boil* is a boil where large bubbles are moving fiercely over the surface of the water, frothing at the edges. In a gentle boil, the bubbles are smaller, less frequent, and do not froth.

**Coulis**

A sauce made of puréed fruit or vegetables.

**Chopped**

Food that has been cut into small, bite-sized pieces.

**Diced**

Food that has been cut into small cubes.

## Emulsion

When one liquid that would not usually mix with another is mixed together by suspending tiny droplets of the one in the other. The most common mixtures are fat suspended in water, or water suspended in fat. Vinaigrette, mayonnaise, and hollandaise are all examples of emulsions.

## Fold

To combine one mixture into another with a spatula or spoon. Unlike beating or mixing, folding is done with a light touch, usually to keep foam or air trapped in the mixture. To fold, push the spatula into the mix, scrape the bottom of the bowl from below, and "fold" the mixture over itself. Repeat until combined, but don't over-mix.

## Heavy cream

Cream with a high fat content is said to be *heavy*. Also known as Whipping Cream and Double Cream. Because it's the fat that prevents the cream from curdling, do not substitute with low-fat varieties.

## Julienne

Food that has been cut into long, thin sticks.

## Minced

Food that has been cut into very small, tiny pieces. Minced food is cut into much smaller pieces than chopped food is.

## Pan fry

Pan frying is a method of cooking where you rapidly heat ingredients in a shallow pan with a small amount of oil. It is related to but not the same as deep frying, where you submerge the ingredients in hot oil to cook them.

## Poach

To cook in a boiling or simmering liquid.

## Pulse

To pulse in a blender or food processor is to blend for short bursts of about 1 second, pausing in between each burst so that the ingredients recombine.

## Reduce

To reduce a liquid is to boil it so that the water in the mixture evaporates, concentrating and thickening the remaining ingredients.

## Roux

A roux is made with flour and fat, and is used as a thickener for sauces. Use equal parts flour and butter as an easy ratio.

## Salt

Seems straight forward enough, right? Actually, there are many kinds of salt, all with slightly different flavors. I recommend having one fine salt for baking and salting water, and one coarse seasoning salt (like kosher salt or sea salt) for seasoning sauces and sprinkling on dishes.

## Sauté

Sauté comes from the French word sauter: *to jump*. To get what you're cooking jumping, you must be using high heat. Because you are using high heat, you also want to keep your food moving - jumping, you could say - around in the pan. Sautéing requires constant attention, so don't walk away from the food when cooking this way.

## Simmer

To cook over a low flame so that any liquids in the pan are just brought to bubbling.

## Split

When a sauce "splits", the emulsified mixture of fat and water separate. This may happen to sauces in which oil or butter is suspended in a liquid mixture, particularly during temperature extremes. To re-emulsify a split sauce, follow the instructions in **Storage and Reheating of Sauces**.

## Zest

Zest is the outer part of the peel of a citrus fruit, like an orange or a lemon. The peel is made up of two layers, the outer zest and the bitter white pith underneath. Zest contains citrus oils but not the acidity of the fruit's juice, so it can be used without curdling dairy products as well as to stand up to the temperatures of baking.

**Have a question? Suggestions? A recipe you want to see?**

Check out The Homemade Cook on Facebook at

http://www.facebook.com/TheHomemadeCook

for more recipes, tips, and sauces!

# HAPPY COOKING!

# Recommended Reading

Mastering the Art of French Cooking, 40th Anniversary Edition

by Julia Child

Barefoot in Paris: Easy French Food You Can Make at Home

by Ina Garten

Essential Pepin: More Than 700 All-Time Favorites from My Life in Food

by Jacques Pepin

The French Laundry Cookbook

by Thomas Keller

Around My French Table: More Than 300 Recipes from My Home to Yours

by Dorie Greenspan